Cricket Training Log and Diary

This Book Belongs To:

_____

DATE: **WEEK:**   **HOURS TRAINED:**

COACH: **TIME:**

GOALS

WARM UP/ DRILLS

TECHNIQUE 1

TECHNIQUE 2

NOTES

DATE: WEEK: **HOURS TRAINED:**

COACH: **TIME:**

GOALS

WARM UP/ DRILLS

TECHNIQUE 1

TECHNIQUE 2

NOTES

DATE: **WEEK:**   **HOURS TRAINED:**

COACH: **TIME:**

GOALS

WARM UP/ DRILLS

TECHNIQUE 1

TECHNIQUE 2

NOTES

DATE: **WEEK:** **HOURS TRAINED:**

COACH: **TIME:**

GOALS

WARM UP/ DRILLS

TECHNIQUE 1

TECHNIQUE 2

NOTES

DATE: ☐ **WEEK:** ☐ **HOURS TRAINED:** ☐

COACH: ☐ **TIME:** ☐

GOALS

WARM UP/ DRILLS

TECHNIQUE 1

TECHNIQUE 2

NOTES

DATE: **WEEK:** **HOURS TRAINED:**

COACH: **TIME:**

GOALS

WARM UP/ DRILLS

TECHNIQUE 1

TECHNIQUE 2

NOTES

DATE: _____ **WEEK:** _____ **HOURS TRAINED:** _____

COACH: _____ **TIME:** _____

GOALS

WARM UP/ DRILLS

TECHNIQUE 1

TECHNIQUE 2

NOTES

DATE: **WEEK:** **HOURS TRAINED:**

COACH: **TIME:**

GOALS

WARM UP/ DRILLS

TECHNIQUE 1

TECHNIQUE 2

NOTES

DATE: _____ **WEEK:** _____ **HOURS TRAINED:** _____

COACH: _____ **TIME:** _____

GOALS

WARM UP/ DRILLS

TECHNIQUE 1

TECHNIQUE 2

NOTES

DATE: _____ **WEEK:** _____ **HOURS TRAINED:** _____

COACH: _____ **TIME:** _____

GOALS

WARM UP/ DRILLS

TECHNIQUE 1

TECHNIQUE 2

NOTES

DATE: [_____]   **WEEK:** [_____]   **HOURS TRAINED:** [_____]

COACH: [_____]   **TIME:** [_____]

GOALS

WARM UP/ DRILLS

TECHNIQUE 1

TECHNIQUE 2

NOTES

DATE:

WEEK:

HOURS TRAINED:

COACH:

TIME:

GOALS

WARM UP/ DRILLS

TECHNIQUE 1

TECHNIQUE 2

NOTES

DATE: _____ **WEEK:** _____ **HOURS TRAINED:** _____

COACH: _____ **TIME:** _____

GOALS

WARM UP/ DRILLS

TECHNIQUE 1

TECHNIQUE 2

NOTES

DATE: | **WEEK:** | **HOURS TRAINED:**

COACH: | **TIME:**

GOALS

WARM UP/ DRILLS

TECHNIQUE 1

TECHNIQUE 2

NOTES

DATE: _____ **WEEK:** _____ **HOURS TRAINED:** _____

COACH: _____ **TIME:** _____

GOALS

WARM UP/ DRILLS

TECHNIQUE 1

TECHNIQUE 2

NOTES

DATE: _____ **WEEK:** _____ **HOURS TRAINED:** _____

COACH: _____ **TIME:** _____

GOALS

WARM UP/ DRILLS

TECHNIQUE 1

TECHNIQUE 2

NOTES

DATE: _____ **WEEK:** _____ **HOURS TRAINED:** _____

COACH: _____ **TIME:** _____

GOALS

WARM UP/ DRILLS

TECHNIQUE 1

TECHNIQUE 2

NOTES

DATE: _____ **WEEK:** _____ **HOURS TRAINED:** _____

COACH: _____ **TIME:** _____

GOALS

WARM UP/ DRILLS

TECHNIQUE 1

TECHNIQUE 2

NOTES

DATE: **WEEK:** **HOURS TRAINED:**

COACH: **TIME:**

GOALS

WARM UP/ DRILLS

TECHNIQUE 1

TECHNIQUE 2

NOTES

DATE: **WEEK:** **HOURS TRAINED:**

COACH: **TIME:**

GOALS

WARM UP/ DRILLS

TECHNIQUE 1

TECHNIQUE 2

NOTES

DATE: ☐ **WEEK:** ☐ **HOURS TRAINED:** ☐

COACH: ☐ **TIME:** ☐

GOALS

WARM UP/ DRILLS

TECHNIQUE 1

TECHNIQUE 2

NOTES

DATE: [   ] **WEEK:** [   ] **HOURS TRAINED:** [   ]

COACH: [   ] **TIME:** [   ]

GOALS

WARM UP/ DRILLS

TECHNIQUE 1

TECHNIQUE 2

NOTES

DATE: **WEEK:** **HOURS TRAINED:**

COACH: **TIME:**

GOALS

WARM UP/ DRILLS

TECHNIQUE 1

TECHNIQUE 2

NOTES

DATE: [   ] **WEEK:** [   ] **HOURS TRAINED:** [   ]

COACH: [   ] **TIME:** [   ]

GOALS

WARM UP/ DRILLS

TECHNIQUE 1

TECHNIQUE 2

NOTES

DATE: **WEEK:**   **HOURS TRAINED:**

COACH: **TIME:**

GOALS

WARM UP/ DRILLS

TECHNIQUE 1

TECHNIQUE 2

NOTES

DATE: **WEEK:** **HOURS TRAINED:**

COACH: **TIME:**

GOALS

WARM UP/ DRILLS

TECHNIQUE 1

TECHNIQUE 2

NOTES

DATE: | **WEEK:** | **HOURS TRAINED:**

COACH: | **TIME:**

GOALS

WARM UP/ DRILLS

TECHNIQUE 1

TECHNIQUE 2

NOTES

DATE: _____ **WEEK:** _____ **HOURS TRAINED:** _____

COACH: _____ **TIME:** _____

GOALS

WARM UP/ DRILLS

TECHNIQUE 1

TECHNIQUE 2

NOTES

DATE: _____ **WEEK:** _____ **HOURS TRAINED:** _____

COACH: _____ **TIME:** _____

GOALS

WARM UP/ DRILLS

TECHNIQUE 1

TECHNIQUE 2

NOTES

DATE: **WEEK:** **HOURS TRAINED:**

COACH: **TIME:**

GOALS

WARM UP/ DRILLS

TECHNIQUE 1

TECHNIQUE 2

NOTES

DATE: _____ **WEEK:** _____ **HOURS TRAINED:** _____

COACH: _____ **TIME:** _____

GOALS

WARM UP/ DRILLS

TECHNIQUE 1

TECHNIQUE 2

NOTES

DATE: [ ] **WEEK:** [ ] **HOURS TRAINED:** [ ]

COACH: [ ] **TIME:** [ ]

GOALS

WARM UP/ DRILLS

TECHNIQUE 1

TECHNIQUE 2

NOTES

DATE: _____ **WEEK:** _____ **HOURS TRAINED:** _____

COACH: _____ **TIME:** _____

GOALS

WARM UP/ DRILLS

TECHNIQUE 1

TECHNIQUE 2

NOTES

DATE: **WEEK:** **HOURS TRAINED:**

COACH: **TIME:**

GOALS

WARM UP/ DRILLS

TECHNIQUE 1

TECHNIQUE 2

NOTES

DATE: **WEEK:** **HOURS TRAINED:**

COACH: **TIME:**

GOALS

WARM UP/ DRILLS

TECHNIQUE 1

TECHNIQUE 2

NOTES

DATE: **WEEK:** **HOURS TRAINED:**

COACH: **TIME:**

GOALS

WARM UP/ DRILLS

TECHNIQUE 1

TECHNIQUE 2

NOTES

DATE: _____ **WEEK:** _____ **HOURS TRAINED:** _____

COACH: _____ **TIME:** _____

GOALS

WARM UP/ DRILLS

TECHNIQUE 1

TECHNIQUE 2

NOTES

DATE: _____ **WEEK:** _____ **HOURS TRAINED:** _____

COACH: _____ **TIME:** _____

GOALS

WARM UP/ DRILLS

TECHNIQUE 1

TECHNIQUE 2

NOTES

DATE: **WEEK:**   **HOURS TRAINED:**

COACH: **TIME:**

GOALS

WARM UP/ DRILLS

TECHNIQUE 1

TECHNIQUE 2

NOTES

DATE: _____ **WEEK:** _____ **HOURS TRAINED:** _____

COACH: _____ **TIME:** _____

GOALS

WARM UP/ DRILLS

TECHNIQUE 1

TECHNIQUE 2

NOTES

DATE: _____ **WEEK:** _____ **HOURS TRAINED:** _____

COACH: _____ **TIME:** _____

GOALS

WARM UP/ DRILLS

TECHNIQUE 1

TECHNIQUE 2

NOTES

DATE: [ ] **WEEK:** [ ] **HOURS TRAINED:** [ ]

COACH: [ ] **TIME:** [ ]

GOALS

WARM UP/ DRILLS

TECHNIQUE 1

TECHNIQUE 2

NOTES

DATE: **WEEK:**   **HOURS TRAINED:**

COACH: **TIME:**

GOALS

WARM UP/ DRILLS

TECHNIQUE 1

TECHNIQUE 2

NOTES

DATE: **WEEK:**   **HOURS TRAINED:**

COACH: **TIME:**

GOALS

WARM UP/ DRILLS

TECHNIQUE 1

TECHNIQUE 2

NOTES

DATE: | **WEEK:** | **HOURS TRAINED:**

COACH: | **TIME:**

GOALS

WARM UP/ DRILLS

TECHNIQUE 1

TECHNIQUE 2

NOTES

DATE: _____ **WEEK:** _____ **HOURS TRAINED:** _____

COACH: _____ **TIME:** _____

GOALS

WARM UP/ DRILLS

TECHNIQUE 1

TECHNIQUE 2

NOTES

DATE: _____ **WEEK:** _____ **HOURS TRAINED:** _____

COACH: _____ **TIME:** _____

GOALS

WARM UP/ DRILLS

TECHNIQUE 1

TECHNIQUE 2

NOTES

DATE: _____   **WEEK:** _____   **HOURS TRAINED:** _____

COACH: _____   **TIME:** _____

GOALS

WARM UP/ DRILLS

TECHNIQUE 1

TECHNIQUE 2

NOTES

DATE: _____ **WEEK:** _____ **HOURS TRAINED:** _____

COACH: _____ **TIME:** _____

GOALS

WARM UP/ DRILLS

TECHNIQUE 1

TECHNIQUE 2

NOTES

DATE: **WEEK:**   **HOURS TRAINED:**

COACH: **TIME:**

GOALS

WARM UP/ DRILLS

TECHNIQUE 1

TECHNIQUE 2

NOTES

DATE: _____ **WEEK:** _____ **HOURS TRAINED:** _____

COACH: _____ **TIME:** _____

GOALS

WARM UP/ DRILLS

TECHNIQUE 1

TECHNIQUE 2

NOTES

DATE: _____ **WEEK:** _____ **HOURS TRAINED:** _____

COACH: _____ **TIME:** _____

GOALS

WARM UP/ DRILLS

TECHNIQUE 1

TECHNIQUE 2

NOTES

DATE: _____ **WEEK:** _____ **HOURS TRAINED:** _____

COACH: _____ **TIME:** _____

GOALS

WARM UP/ DRILLS

TECHNIQUE 1

TECHNIQUE 2

NOTES

DATE: **WEEK:** **HOURS TRAINED:**

COACH: **TIME:**

GOALS

WARM UP/ DRILLS

TECHNIQUE 1

TECHNIQUE 2

NOTES

DATE: _____ **WEEK:** _____ **HOURS TRAINED:** _____

COACH: _____ **TIME:** _____

GOALS

WARM UP/ DRILLS

TECHNIQUE 1

TECHNIQUE 2

NOTES

DATE: **WEEK:** **HOURS TRAINED:**

COACH: **TIME:**

GOALS

WARM UP/ DRILLS

TECHNIQUE 1

TECHNIQUE 2

NOTES

DATE: _____ **WEEK:** _____ **HOURS TRAINED:** _____

COACH: _____ **TIME:** _____

GOALS

WARM UP/ DRILLS

TECHNIQUE 1

TECHNIQUE 2

NOTES

DATE: _____   **WEEK:** _____   **HOURS TRAINED:** _____

COACH: _____   **TIME:** _____

GOALS

WARM UP/ DRILLS

TECHNIQUE 1

TECHNIQUE 2

NOTES

DATE: _____ **WEEK:** _____ **HOURS TRAINED:** _____

COACH: _____ **TIME:** _____

GOALS

WARM UP/ DRILLS

TECHNIQUE 1

TECHNIQUE 2

NOTES

DATE: [ ]   **WEEK:** [ ]   **HOURS TRAINED:** [ ]

COACH: [ ]   **TIME:** [ ]

GOALS

WARM UP/ DRILLS

TECHNIQUE 1

TECHNIQUE 2

NOTES

DATE: _____ **WEEK:** _____ **HOURS TRAINED:** _____

COACH: _____ **TIME:** _____

GOALS

WARM UP/ DRILLS

TECHNIQUE 1

TECHNIQUE 2

NOTES

DATE: **WEEK:**   **HOURS TRAINED:**

COACH: **TIME:**

GOALS

WARM UP/ DRILLS

TECHNIQUE 1

TECHNIQUE 2

NOTES

DATE: _____ **WEEK:** _____ **HOURS TRAINED:** _____

COACH: _____ **TIME:** _____

GOALS

WARM UP/ DRILLS

TECHNIQUE 1

TECHNIQUE 2

NOTES

DATE: _____ **WEEK:** _____ **HOURS TRAINED:** _____

COACH: _____ **TIME:** _____

GOALS

WARM UP/ DRILLS

TECHNIQUE 1

TECHNIQUE 2

NOTES

DATE: [ ] **WEEK:** [ ] **HOURS TRAINED:** [ ]

COACH: [ ] **TIME:** [ ]

GOALS

WARM UP/ DRILLS

TECHNIQUE 1

TECHNIQUE 2

NOTES

DATE: **WEEK:** **HOURS TRAINED:**

COACH: **TIME:**

GOALS

WARM UP/ DRILLS

TECHNIQUE 1

TECHNIQUE 2

NOTES

DATE: | **WEEK:** | **HOURS TRAINED:**

COACH: | **TIME:**

GOALS

WARM UP/ DRILLS

TECHNIQUE 1

TECHNIQUE 2

NOTES

DATE: **WEEK:** **HOURS TRAINED:**

COACH: **TIME:**

GOALS

WARM UP/ DRILLS

TECHNIQUE 1

TECHNIQUE 2

NOTES

DATE: **WEEK:**   **HOURS TRAINED:**

COACH: **TIME:**

GOALS

WARM UP/ DRILLS

TECHNIQUE 1

TECHNIQUE 2

NOTES

DATE: **WEEK:**   **HOURS TRAINED:**

COACH: **TIME:**

GOALS

WARM UP/ DRILLS

TECHNIQUE 1

TECHNIQUE 2

NOTES

DATE: _____   **WEEK:** _____   **HOURS TRAINED:** _____

COACH: _____   **TIME:** _____

GOALS

WARM UP/ DRILLS

TECHNIQUE 1

TECHNIQUE 2

NOTES

DATE: _____ **WEEK:** _____ **HOURS TRAINED:** _____

COACH: _____ **TIME:** _____

GOALS

WARM UP/ DRILLS

TECHNIQUE 1

TECHNIQUE 2

NOTES

DATE: **WEEK:** **HOURS TRAINED:**

COACH: **TIME:**

GOALS

WARM UP/ DRILLS

TECHNIQUE 1

TECHNIQUE 2

NOTES

DATE: **WEEK:** **HOURS TRAINED:**

COACH: **TIME:**

GOALS

WARM UP/ DRILLS

TECHNIQUE 1

TECHNIQUE 2

NOTES

DATE: _____ **WEEK:** _____ **HOURS TRAINED:** _____

COACH: _____ **TIME:** _____

GOALS

WARM UP/ DRILLS

TECHNIQUE 1

TECHNIQUE 2

NOTES

DATE: **WEEK:** **HOURS TRAINED:**

COACH: **TIME:**

GOALS

WARM UP/ DRILLS

TECHNIQUE 1

TECHNIQUE 2

NOTES

DATE: _____ **WEEK:** _____ **HOURS TRAINED:** _____

COACH: _____   **TIME:** _____

GOALS

WARM UP/ DRILLS

TECHNIQUE 1

TECHNIQUE 2

NOTES

DATE: **WEEK:**   **HOURS TRAINED:**

COACH: **TIME:**

GOALS

WARM UP/ DRILLS

TECHNIQUE 1

TECHNIQUE 2

NOTES

DATE: _____ **WEEK:** _____ **HOURS TRAINED:** _____

COACH: _____ **TIME:** _____

GOALS

WARM UP/ DRILLS

TECHNIQUE 1

TECHNIQUE 2

NOTES

DATE: _____ **WEEK:** _____ **HOURS TRAINED:** _____

COACH: _____ **TIME:** _____

GOALS

WARM UP/ DRILLS

TECHNIQUE 1

TECHNIQUE 2

NOTES

DATE: **WEEK:** **HOURS TRAINED:**

COACH: **TIME:**

GOALS

WARM UP/ DRILLS

TECHNIQUE 1

TECHNIQUE 2

NOTES

DATE: **WEEK:** **HOURS TRAINED:**

COACH: **TIME:**

GOALS

WARM UP/ DRILLS

TECHNIQUE 1

TECHNIQUE 2

NOTES

DATE: _____ **WEEK:** _____ **HOURS TRAINED:** _____

COACH: _____ **TIME:** _____

GOALS

WARM UP/ DRILLS

TECHNIQUE 1

TECHNIQUE 2

NOTES

DATE: | **WEEK:** | **HOURS TRAINED:**

COACH: | **TIME:**

GOALS

WARM UP/ DRILLS

TECHNIQUE 1

TECHNIQUE 2

NOTES

DATE: _____ **WEEK:** _____ **HOURS TRAINED:** _____

COACH: _____ **TIME:** _____

GOALS

WARM UP/ DRILLS

TECHNIQUE 1

TECHNIQUE 2

NOTES

DATE: **WEEK:** **HOURS TRAINED:**

COACH: **TIME:**

GOALS

WARM UP/ DRILLS

TECHNIQUE 1

TECHNIQUE 2

NOTES

DATE: _____ **WEEK:** _____ **HOURS TRAINED:** _____

COACH: _____ **TIME:** _____

GOALS

WARM UP/ DRILLS

TECHNIQUE 1

TECHNIQUE 2

NOTES

DATE: _____ **WEEK:** _____ **HOURS TRAINED:** _____

COACH: _____ **TIME:** _____

GOALS

WARM UP/ DRILLS

TECHNIQUE 1

TECHNIQUE 2

NOTES

DATE: _____ **WEEK:** _____ **HOURS TRAINED:** _____

COACH: _____ **TIME:** _____

GOALS

WARM UP/ DRILLS

TECHNIQUE 1

TECHNIQUE 2

NOTES

DATE: _____ **WEEK:** _____ **HOURS TRAINED:** _____

COACH: _____ **TIME:** _____

GOALS

WARM UP/ DRILLS

TECHNIQUE 1

TECHNIQUE 2

NOTES

DATE: | **WEEK:** | **HOURS TRAINED:**

COACH: | **TIME:**

GOALS

WARM UP/ DRILLS

TECHNIQUE 1

TECHNIQUE 2

NOTES

DATE: [   ] **WEEK:** [   ] **HOURS TRAINED:** [   ]

COACH: [   ] **TIME:** [   ]

GOALS

WARM UP/ DRILLS

TECHNIQUE 1

TECHNIQUE 2

NOTES

DATE: _____ **WEEK:** _____ **HOURS TRAINED:** _____

COACH: _____ **TIME:** _____

GOALS

WARM UP/ DRILLS

TECHNIQUE 1

TECHNIQUE 2

NOTES

DATE: _____ **WEEK:** _____ **HOURS TRAINED:** _____

COACH: _____ **TIME:** _____

GOALS

WARM UP/ DRILLS

TECHNIQUE 1

TECHNIQUE 2

NOTES

DATE: **WEEK:** **HOURS TRAINED:**

COACH: **TIME:**

GOALS

WARM UP/ DRILLS

TECHNIQUE 1

TECHNIQUE 2

NOTES

DATE: _____ **WEEK:** _____ **HOURS TRAINED:** _____

COACH: _____ **TIME:** _____

GOALS

WARM UP/ DRILLS

TECHNIQUE 1

TECHNIQUE 2

NOTES

DATE: _____ **WEEK:** _____ **HOURS TRAINED:** _____

COACH: _____ **TIME:** _____

GOALS

WARM UP/ DRILLS

TECHNIQUE 1

TECHNIQUE 2

NOTES

DATE: **WEEK:** **HOURS TRAINED:**

COACH: **TIME:**

GOALS

WARM UP/ DRILLS

TECHNIQUE 1

TECHNIQUE 2

NOTES

DATE: **WEEK:**   **HOURS TRAINED:**

COACH: **TIME:**

GOALS

WARM UP/ DRILLS

TECHNIQUE 1

TECHNIQUE 2

NOTES

DATE: _____   **WEEK:** _____   **HOURS TRAINED:** _____

COACH: _____   **TIME:** _____

GOALS

WARM UP/ DRILLS

TECHNIQUE 1

TECHNIQUE 2

NOTES

DATE: **WEEK:** **HOURS TRAINED:**

COACH: **TIME:**

GOALS

WARM UP/ DRILLS

TECHNIQUE 1

TECHNIQUE 2

NOTES

DATE: **WEEK:** **HOURS TRAINED:**

COACH: **TIME:**

GOALS

WARM UP/ DRILLS

TECHNIQUE 1

TECHNIQUE 2

NOTES

DATE: _____   **WEEK:** _____   **HOURS TRAINED:** _____

COACH: _____   **TIME:** _____

GOALS

WARM UP/ DRILLS

TECHNIQUE 1

TECHNIQUE 2

NOTES

DATE: _____ **WEEK:** _____ **HOURS TRAINED:** _____

COACH: _____ **TIME:** _____

GOALS

WARM UP/ DRILLS

TECHNIQUE 1

TECHNIQUE 2

NOTES

DATE: **WEEK:** **HOURS TRAINED:**

COACH: **TIME:**

GOALS

WARM UP/ DRILLS

TECHNIQUE 1

TECHNIQUE 2

NOTES

DATE: | **WEEK:** | **HOURS TRAINED:**

COACH: | **TIME:**

GOALS

WARM UP/ DRILLS

TECHNIQUE 1

TECHNIQUE 2

NOTES

DATE: _____ **WEEK:** ___ **HOURS TRAINED:** _____

COACH: _____ **TIME:** _____

GOALS

WARM UP/ DRILLS

TECHNIQUE 1

TECHNIQUE 2

NOTES

DATE: | **WEEK:** | **HOURS TRAINED:**

COACH: | **TIME:**

GOALS

WARM UP/ DRILLS

TECHNIQUE 1

TECHNIQUE 2

NOTES

DATE: _____ **WEEK:** _____ **HOURS TRAINED:** _____

COACH: _____ **TIME:** _____

GOALS

WARM UP/ DRILLS

TECHNIQUE 1

TECHNIQUE 2

NOTES

DATE: _____ **WEEK:** _____ **HOURS TRAINED:** _____

COACH: _____ **TIME:** _____

GOALS

WARM UP/ DRILLS

TECHNIQUE 1

TECHNIQUE 2

NOTES

DATE: _____ **WEEK:** _____ **HOURS TRAINED:** _____

COACH: _____ **TIME:** _____

GOALS

WARM UP/ DRILLS

TECHNIQUE 1

TECHNIQUE 2

NOTES

DATE: **WEEK:** **HOURS TRAINED:**

COACH: **TIME:**

GOALS

WARM UP/ DRILLS

TECHNIQUE 1

TECHNIQUE 2

NOTES

DATE: | **WEEK:** | **HOURS TRAINED:**

COACH: | **TIME:**

GOALS

WARM UP/ DRILLS

TECHNIQUE 1

TECHNIQUE 2

NOTES

DATE: **WEEK:** **HOURS TRAINED:**

COACH: **TIME:**

GOALS

WARM UP/ DRILLS

TECHNIQUE 1

TECHNIQUE 2

NOTES

DATE: **WEEK:**   **HOURS TRAINED:**

COACH: **TIME:**

GOALS

WARM UP/ DRILLS

TECHNIQUE 1

TECHNIQUE 2

NOTES

DATE: **WEEK:** **HOURS TRAINED:**

COACH: **TIME:**

GOALS

WARM UP/ DRILLS

TECHNIQUE 1

TECHNIQUE 2

NOTES

DATE: **WEEK:** **HOURS TRAINED:**

COACH: **TIME:**

GOALS

WARM UP/ DRILLS

TECHNIQUE 1

TECHNIQUE 2

NOTES

DATE: **WEEK:**   **HOURS TRAINED:**

COACH: **TIME:**

GOALS

WARM UP/ DRILLS

TECHNIQUE 1

TECHNIQUE 2

NOTES

DATE: _____ **WEEK:** _____ **HOURS TRAINED:** _____

COACH: _____ **TIME:** _____

GOALS

WARM UP/ DRILLS

TECHNIQUE 1

TECHNIQUE 2

NOTES

Printed in Great Britain
by Amazon

34397849R00070